Walther Ziegler

Camus
in 60 Minutes

Translated by
Alexander Reynolds

My thanks go to Rudolf Aichner for his tireless critical editing; Silke Ruthenberg for the fine graphics; Lydia Pointvogl, Eva Amberger, Christiane Hüttner, and Dr. Martin Engler for their excellent work as manuscript readers and sub-editors; Prof. Guntram Knapp, who first inspired me with enthusiasm for philosophy; and Angela Schumitz, who handled in the most professional manner, as chief editorial reader, the production of both the German and the English editions of this series of books.

My special thanks go to my translator

Dr Alexander Reynolds.

Himself a philosopher, he not only translated the original German text into English with great care and precision but also, in passages where this was required in order to ensure clear understanding, supplemented this text with certain formulations adapted specifically to the needs of English-language readers.

Bibliographic Information held by the German National Library: The details of the original German edition of this publication are held by the German National Library as part of the German National Bibliography; detailed bibliographical data can be found online at www.dnb.de.

© 2016 Dr Walther Ziegler
1st Edition June 2016
Jacket design and graphic design for the whole book: Silke Ruthenberg, making use of illustrations by:
Raphael Bräsecke, Creactive – Studio for Advertising, Comics & Illustrations
© JackF - Fotolia.com (image-frames)
© Valerie Potapova - Fotolia.com (image-frames)
© Svetlana Gryankina - Fotolia.com (speech-balloons)

Publisher and Printing:
BoD – Books on Demand, Norderstedt
ISBN 9783741227738

Contents

Camus' Great Discovery — 7

Camus' Central Idea — 13
- The Sense of Absurdity — 13
- Suicide as an Evasion of Absurdity — 26
- Religion – the Second Attempt to Evade Absurdity — 31
- Ideology – the Third Attempt to Evade Absurdity — 35
- Honesty with Oneself in the Face of Absurdity — 39
- The Myth of Sisyphus — 43
- Rebellion as an Attitude to Life — 47

Of What Use is Camus' Discovery for Us Today? — 53
- Living With Absurdity – Freeing Oneself from Bourgeois Rules of Conduct — 53
- Absurd Lifestyles: Actors and Seducers — 58
- Finding the "Golden Mean" — 64
- Composure in the Face of Life's Unpredictability — 67

Bibliographical References: — 75

Camus' Great Discovery

The philosophical discovery made by Albert Camus (1913-1960) is, even today, a provocative one. For, like all great philosophers, Camus posed the question: 'What is the meaning of life?' But the answer he gave to this question was of a new sort entirely.

Different answers have been given, of course, down the ages to this question of 'the meaning of life'. For Plato it is 'the Good' that holds the world together; for Hegel the 'World-Spirit'; for Marx class struggle; for Sartre freedom; for Nietzsche 'will to power'; and for Habermas the development of communicative reason. In fact, each philosopher has his own answer to this question. But Camus is the exception here. He has none. Or rather, worse: he has an answer, but one of very sobering effect. His answer to the question 'what is the meaning of life?' is simply 'It has no meaning. Life is absurd':

It is a matter of living in that state of the absurd.[2]

But Camus would not have been a philosopher if he had been content just to register life's meaninglessness. He in fact not only backed up his pessimistic judgment with many examples but took this absurdity of the world as the starting point for a whole series of interesting reflections. He posed, for example, the radical question of whether, given the world's absurdity, the only consistent course of action is to take one's own life: Is suicide the logical conclusion to be drawn from the experience of meaninglessness? Or must one rather carry on living in and with the feeling of absurdity? And if so – how is one to go about this?

Camus answers these questions in his two main philosophical works, *The Myth of Sisyphus* and *The Rebel*. Both books are written in an expansive, essayistic style quite distinct from the dry, analytic writing of most classical philosophers. Camus, indeed, saw himself more as a literary man than as a philosopher. Thus, we see his experience of the absurd reflected also in his novels, for which he received the Nobel Prize for Literature in 1959. In the novel *The Outsider* Camus shows in masterly fashion how a single chance encounter on a beach can completely alter a human life and throw it off course in just a few seconds. But the discovery of absurdity and the conclusions that he draws from it definitely do have a philosophical core. Camus counts, together with Sartre and Heidegger, as one of the most important representatives of philosophical existentialism.

He was born in 1913 in the French colony, Algeria. His father worked as a cellarman and his mother in a factory. In 1939, the 26-year-old North African was deeply marked by the outbreak of the Second World War. It seemed incomprehensible to him that, after the experiences of the First World War, humanity could once again plunge into such slaughter. Bewildered he noted the striking contradiction between the news that war had broken out and the persistence of "the blue sky over the sea" and "the humming of the cicadas". Camus felt at a loss to align, in his mind, the approaching catastrophe with the enduring beauty of Nature:

War has broken out. But where is it? [...] Where does this absurd event show itself, except in the news bulletins we have to believe and the notices we have to read?[3]

His consternation at the outbreak of war may well have sharpened Camus' sense for the absurd but the revealing of this aspect of human life had from the start for Camus something timeless. Camus' philosophical problem was, in the last analysis, that of the search for meaning in a chaotic, ungraspable world. Because the world that surrounds us and in which we move is, Camus says, full of surprises. It cannot be controlled; it is random and irrational. Man, however, has always striven after order. He is afraid of a future that lies beyond his power to plan and dispose and would like, ideally, to be able to understand, logically explain, and thereby precisely predict all that confronts or will confront him. It is this experience of the irreconcilability of his inner need for order with the real outer world that necessarily gives rise to Man's sense of absurdity:

[...] What is absurd is the confrontation of the irrational and the wild longing for clarity whose call echoes in the human heart.[4]

The problem Camus raises here of a lack of orientation in the world is in fact very topical even today, more than fifty years after his death. In Europe and large areas of the Western world religious belief is declining in importance. Fewer and fewer people believe in God or life after death. Religion seems no longer to function as a source of meaning. People today face the great task of mastering their lives through their own resources alone. Particularly now that the material utopias of a future classless society seem also to have failed, the 'meaning question' faces us today with especial gravity.

To the question 'how should I live?' Camus gives an answer of dazzling originality: one must learn to deal with the fact of absurdity. One must not repress or try to deaden the feeling of absurdity but rather nurture it. As Camus puts it, one must "keep the absurd alive":

Living is keeping the absurd alive. Keeping it alive is above all contemplating it.[5]

His reflections on how best to confront absurdity and form a life for oneself without God and without ideological orientation are more relevant today than they ever were. Camus' great achievement, then, was not so much the discovery of the sense of absurdity and of the meaninglessness of life as the discovery of the various ways in which we can deal with this meaninglessness.

Camus' Central Idea

The Sense of Absurdity

Absurdity, for Camus, is not the result of conscious reflection or rational analysis but rather a feeling – one which always arises when one's familiar daily routine collapses:

> It happens that the stage sets collapse. Rising, streetcar, four hours in the office or factory, meal, streetcar, four hours of work, meal, sleep, and Monday, Tuesday, Wednesday, Thursday, Friday, Saturday, according to the same rhythm – this path is easily followed most of the time. But one day the 'why' arises and everything begins in that weariness tinged with amazement. 'Begins' – this is important.[6]

Because once a human being has begun to doubt the world he is accustomed to he will never again be completely absorbed and subsumed in it. Once the experience of absurdity has arisen, it will never again release its grip on him. The direct perception of absurdity can be awoken by individual feelings or events. If, for example, a relationship breaks down and you lose a partner whose love and devotion you believed were yours forever, this often renders fragile and uncertain all the other aspects of your life as well. Everything in which one had, so recently, had an implicit trust now seems strange and absurd. One suddenly notices that all the things that one had formerly looked on as real and objective were in fact things that one had merely read into it:

> For a second we cease to understand (the world) because for centuries we have understood in it only the images and designs that we had attributed to it beforehand, because henceforth we lack the power to make use of that artifice. The world evades us because it becomes itself again.[7]

Camus' Central Idea

The romantic, old-world style apartment, for example, that we had shared with our departed partner; the restaurants and little squares which had once so warmly received us – all these things suddenly become again what they really were all along: anonymous and unconcerned with us. The romantic movies on TV seem false to us now and even the woodland paths on which we'd walked and all the rest of Nature around us suddenly show their true face. That Nature which had seemed a bosom friend reveals, all at once, its utter indifference:

At the heart of all beauty lies something inhuman, and these hills, the softness of the sky, the outline of these trees at this very minute lose the illusory meaning with which we had clothed them, henceforth more remote than a lost paradise.[8]

The diagnosis of a serious illness such as cancer is also apt to awaken the sense of absurdity. The medical explanation here – namely, that the renewal of the body's cells is a perfectly normal process and that cancer cells are simply cells that reproduce beyond the natural rate – is reasonable and comprehensible. But for the person actually affected by it this process of accelerated cell-division is an absurdity that he cannot be reasonably expected to come to terms with. It is impossible to fit the illness into the familiar plan of a life, since it puts everything into question. As Camus insists, however, it is not always such a shaking of our whole existence that is required in order for the absurd to suddenly enter our life:

At any street corner the feeling of absurdity can strike any man in the face.[9]

Many people, for example, will know the strange feeling that arises when one looks down from a church tower onto a busy square. Seen from high above, the people look like nothing more than little black dots.

They run about hectically in different directions like ants, their paths crossing, until they vanish from the scene and their place is taken by others just like them. From this birds-eye view, such restless motion appears laughable, indeed downright absurd. Although each person down on the square probably has a reason for following their route and possibly even an ambitious life-plan, this frenzy of activity, taken in aggregate, gives a disconcerting impression of senselessness. If one of these "ants" were suddenly removed from the scene, by death or otherwise, this would seem unimportant. Its absence from the hurly-burly below would not even be noticed. Observed from so high above, the movements of a single individual seem easily dispensed with – somehow superfluous. This restlessness, these contrary movements, these routes and destinations which are those of one "ant" but could easily be those of another, all appear senseless. All the little concerns and goals which may have, for each individual, such great importance, appear, from a distance, merely random. Relative to the aggregate they amount to nothing and their pursuit seems, to the observer, every second more absurd.

This feeling of the absurd is all the more uncanny because one senses that one is oneself just such an "ant" – just as replaceable and just as insignificant as the others. In the end, one feels oneself to be merely another "dot" moving from A to B – and indeed one day not even moving any more. Camus offers a similar example for this sudden flaring-up of a sense of absurdity in the midst of daily life:

> A man is talking on the telephone behind a glass partition; you cannot hear him but you see his incomprehensible dumb-show: you wonder why he is alive. This discomfort in the face of Man's own inhumanity, this incalculable tumble before the image of what we are, this 'nausea', as a writer of today calls it, is also the absurd.[10]

The sense of absurdity can even seize us in the morning over breakfast, when a familiar person suddenly appears completely strange to us. Camus describes the surreal feeling experienced by a man observing his partner of many years in just this situation. Somehow he is no longer able to perceive her in the accustomed way. Because for a few moments he recalls the woman with whom, many years before, he had fallen in love – who is, however, a woman who cannot be brought, in his mind, to resemble in any way the woman now seated across from him at the breakfast table:

Just as there are days when, under the familiar face of a woman, we see as a stranger her we had loved months or years ago [...].[11]

One feels, of course, initially irritated in such a situation. It is painful to be reminded that one's own wife has become strange to one, and that she is no longer she who she was before. What has become of our beloved? Has she really changed so much? Or is it we who have changed? Why is the mood that pervades our breakfasts together so different? Have we lost all sense for our partner's beauty?

However one might answer such questions, one's accustomed world collapses for a moment. One had been looking forward to the usual pleasant breakfast but, instead of the familiar harmony, one has stumbled – even if it is only for a brief moment – on the strangeness and absurdity of life, on (in Shakespeare's phrase) a "world out of joint". Absurdity can seize us for brief moments in this way – and also for prolonged periods. Indeed, it can become an inner certainty. This is why Camus speaks not just of a "sense of", but also, in many passages, of a "*climate of absurdity*". This climate first subtly implants itself in the hearts of men and only later becomes an attitude of mind:

> The climate of absurdity is in the beginning. The end is the absurd universe and that attitude of mind which lights the world with its true colours to bring out the privileged and implacable visage which that attitude has discerned in it.[12]

As a rule, human beings avoid, as best they can, perceiving absurdity at all and try to move exclusively within the world they feel familiar with. They give a meaning to their life and cling to routines. They structure their daily existence, setting professional and personal goals for themselves for which, if asked, they can give a host of good reasons. But still absurdity can break forth at any time and shake this familiarity to its foundations:

> A world that can be explained even with bad reasons is a familiar world. But, on the other hand, in a universe suddenly divested of illusions and lights, Man feels an alien, a stranger [...] This divorce between Man and his life, the actor and his setting, is properly the feeling of absurdity.[13]

The sense of absurdity always arises, then, when a human being can no longer find his bearings in key aspects of his own life. He feels as though he has been expelled into a strange world. But this feeling of "divorce" from one's world does not arise by chance. It arises, says Camus, necessarily. This is why the experience of absurdity strikes not just some people but all. Each of us will experience at some point this conflict with our world, since the wish for unity, predictability and order is a basic driving force in Man:

That nostalgia for unity, that appetite for the absolute, illustrates the essential impulse for the human drama.[14]

Camus speaks here of a "human drama", that is to say, an unavoidable catastrophe toward which all who are involved in it must slide. Because, whereas the search for meaning must be undertaken, it is nonetheless doomed to fail, since the world is, in the end, chaotic, unpredictable and irrational. Our life is exposed to a thousand chance events: illnesses, accidents, climatic disasters, chance encounters, opportunities seized or missed; and all this stands in constant contradiction to our longing for order and predictability:

> That evidence is the absurd. It is that divorce between the mind that desires and the world that disappoints [...].[15]

The divorce between the mind seeking order and the disappointing world is, Camus says, inevitable, and gives rise to the climate of absurdity:

> This world in itself is not reasonable, that is all that can be said. But what is absurd is the confrontation of the irrational and the wild longing for clarity whose call echoes in the human heart.[16]

The climate of absurdity, then, arises out of the collision between a rational need for order and an irrational world. The sense of absurdity is further sharpened by the certainty that we must one day die. The inevitability of death puts all our efforts to give sense to our lives into question. This, Camus says, is why so many people block out this fact of death as long as possible. Young people certainly don't think of death and live as if they are going to live forever. But even they awaken from this illusion at some point and recognize that it is their fate to be bound to a body that will pass away. As Camus writes:

> Yet a time comes when a man notices or says that he is thirty. Thus he asserts his youth. But simultaneously he situates himself in relation to time. He takes his place in it. [...] He belongs to time and, by the horror that seizes him, he recognizes his worst enemy [...]. This revolt of the flesh is the absurd.[17]

Nothing is so opposed to human nature and our will to live as death is. We are born and wish to live; we are free and yet condemned to die. Death forces people to accept the inconceivable: the limitedness and the absurdity of all our efforts in this world. Whatever grandiose, imaginative projects we may plan to put into practice, at some point we must come to our senses and admit to ourselves that our life's work can only be a fragment:

Hence the intelligence, too, tells me in its way that this world is absurd.[18]

Camus comes to the conclusion that the sense of the absurdity of human life is a comprehensible, indeed unavoidable fact. Many people try to block out all awareness of this fact. But whoever is honest with himself will acknowledge that he is radically exposed to absurdity.

Suicide as an Evasion of Absurdity

If life, then, really has no meaning the question necessarily arises of whether we should not escape this meaninglessness simply by putting an end to our lives. Camus poses this question right at the start of his philosophical investigation. The very first sentence of his famous book *The Myth of Sisyphus* runs:

> There is but one truly serious philosophical problem and that is suicide. Judging whether life is or is not worth living amounts to answering the fundamental question of philosophy.[19]

The question becomes an even graver one when one includes in it the demand that a man's actions must accord with his judgments. A thinker who does indeed judge that life is senseless and absurd would appear, by this logic, to have to draw a correspondingly extreme practical conclusion:

The principle can be established that for a man who does not cheat what he believes to be true must determine his action. Belief in the absurdity of existence must then dictate his conduct. It is legitimate to wonder, clearly and without false pathos, whether a conclusion of this importance requires forsaking as rapidly as possible an incomprehensible condition.[20]

Camus here even puts to himself the question of whether he, as a philosophical representative of absurdity, is not himself logically bound to put an end to his own existence. But on close consideration he concludes that suicide is not in fact the revolt against absurdity that it appears to be:

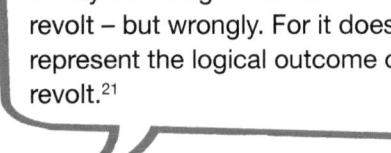

It may be thought that suicide follows revolt – but wrongly. For it does not represent the logical outcome of revolt.[21]

The problem of absurdity, he suggests, is not solved by suicide but merely hidden from view. Suicide is an evasion of absurdity instead of an engagement with it. But it is important, he goes on, to accept absurdity as a challenge:

Living an experience, a particular fate, is accepting it fully. Now, no one will live this fate, knowing it to be absurd, unless he does everything to keep before him that absurd brought to light by consciousness.[22]

Camus' Central Idea

Camus demands of human beings that we be defiantly recalcitrant to the impossible demands placed on us by absurdity, that we carry on living, and that we revolt, each day anew, against meaninglessness. Suicide, he argues, would be a premature and impermissible evasion of this obligation to conscious revolt:

To abolish conscious revolt is to elude the problem.[23]

The absurd, then, must be allowed. Man must engage in a kind of constant revolt or rebellion against the absurd, even if he can never eliminate it:

Living is keeping the absurd alive. Keeping it alive is above all contemplating it.[24]

To "contemplate it", then, does not mean, for Camus, simply to passively accept the meaninglessness of the world and to retreat into resignation. On the contrary, Man can and must try to bring order into the chaos of the world. He will never be able satisfactorily to solve this problem and gain victory in this struggle, but he must nonetheless attempt it day by day. It is his duty to impose some order on the world – even if it is only a temporary order – and to make decisions in the course of everyday life. He must act, even when – indeed precisely when – he is unable to recognize any pre-existing meaning. This is the lived revolt that Camus demands of every individual human being. He describes this daily-renewed struggle as a passionate revolt against the radical exposedness to meaninglessness that is the world:

> That revolt gives life its value [...]. It is essential to die unreconciled and not of one's own free will. Suicide is a repudiation. The absurd man can only drain everything to the bitter end, and deplete himself.[25]

If suicide constitutes an actual physical attempt to evade the task of living with absurdity, this "escape attempt" has its spiritual counterpart in religious faith.

Religion – the Second Attempt to Evade Absurdity

Religion promises Man a life in "the world beyond". It thereby addresses him at just that point where his need for meaning is put under greatest strain and where his sense of absurdity reaches its peak: namely, where he faces death. Religious belief is in fact a response to the absurd reality that we all must die, to which religion opposes the hope of eternal life. To free Man of this terrible emotional and moral strain of death's finality is to make life before death significantly less hard. Life can then be looked on merely as a testing and a preparation for a better afterlife. But to generate meaning through faith has, Camus thinks, two great drawbacks: in the first place, the hope that religion offers is the hope of something that can't be proven; and secondly, it is a hope that robs Man of his dignity and his freedom. Camus explains this first drawback by pointing out that the claim to truth raised by religion is excessive, speculative, and founded in what is openly stated to be "beyond our comprehension":

> It allows one perhaps, as can be seen, to derive hope [...]. But even if fellow-feeling inclines one towards that attitude, still it must be said that excess justifies nothing. That transcends, as the saying goes, the human scale; therefore it must be super-human. But this 'therefore' is superfluous. There is no logical certainty here. There is no experimental probability either.[26]

Camus is a convinced existentialist and atheist. He does not accept, therefore, that human life should be determined by any power situated outside human existence itself. Every thinker, be he theologian or philosopher, whose thinking culminates in the acceptance of a God set above Man commits, according to Camus, "philosophical suicide", since this thinker thereby takes leave of his own self-certainty. This is so inasmuch as, for Camus, human beings have a duty to acquire their knowledge by human means alone:

Camus' Central Idea

> I don't know whether this world has a meaning that transcends it. But I know that I do not know that meaning and that it is impossible for me just now to know it. What can a meaning outside my condition mean to me? I can understand only in human terms.[27]

We must therefore, argues Camus, be satisfied with those things which present themselves to us as evident and certain. And this consists basically in two facts: on the one hand, the longing, present in every human being, for meaning, security, order, and a future that can be planned; on the other hand, the chaotic, unpredictable external world, which stretches us out on the wheel of time and condemns us to death. The irreconcilability of our wish for order with the structural chaos of the world leads over and over again to disappointment and creates what Camus calls a "climate of the absurd".

But even if absurdity is hard to bear, it must be accepted. And on this basis – that is, while acknowledging absurdity – we should attempt to live, to act, and freely to decide. Belief in God, however, would be a denial of our freedom:

> You know the alternative: either we are not free and God the all-powerful is responsible for evil; or we are free and responsible but God is not all-powerful. All the scholastic subtleties have neither added anything to nor subtracted anything from the acuteness of this paradox.[28]

Here Camus addresses the second drawback of religion: belief in God is an evasion of responsibility for one's own self. Camus rejects Christianity's contention that an absolute and all-powerful God has granted Man a little portion of freedom so that he can choose good or evil of his own free will:

> I cannot understand what kind of freedom would be given me by a higher being. I have lost the sense of hierarchy.[29]

Ideology – the Third Attempt to Evade Absurdity

To sum up, then: suicide cannot be a permissible reaction to the absurdity of life since it does not solve the problem of the absurd but only evades it. Religious belief in a meaning given to the world by God is likewise impermissible because, although it relieves the absurd fact of death of its terror, it too is in the end an evasion: namely, of Man's responsibility for himself. The third and final attempt to escape absurdity is the commitment to a political utopia, or the projection of some future ideal society from the perspective of which our absurd present reality can be interpreted merely as a "phase of transition".

Camus criticizes all grand political ideologies which promise Man the achievement of a state of "paradise regained". There is no difference here between the "thousand-year Reich" of the Nazis and the "classless society" of the Marxists: in both cases there is set for humanity some historical goal that lies in the future and that justifies, for the sake of achieving it, every possible sacrifice in the present. But in reality, Camus argues, history has no goal and no recognizable meaning. And even if it were to have a goal, no one can yet say with certainty what that goal is. All those politicians, party leaders and ideologues who insistently claim to know "the final goal of history" are either lying or themselves deluded. In setting a goal that transcends our real, lived lives religion and ideology have this in common:

> Hope of another life one must 'deserve' or trickery of those who live, not for life itself, but for some great idea that will transcend it, refine it, give it a meaning, and betray it.[30]

A philosophy of history which prescribes a meaning for human life is nothing other than a betrayal of this life as human beings actually, concretely live it. Camus' stance here led to a violent polemic with his friend Sartre. Sartre's leftism was one aligned with Marxist ideas and he believed that a classless communist society really was a "goal of history" that could be logically deduced from present economic tendencies. Camus, on the other hand, focussed critically upon the dictatorial "terror" being exercised by communist states during the two men's own lifetimes:

The revolution of the twentieth century [...] claims to base itself on economics but is primarily political and ideological. It cannot, by its very function, avoid terror and violence done to the real. Despite its pretensions, it begins in the absolute and attempts to mould reality.[31]

To propagate the idea of a "final goal of history", Camus argued, amounted to nothing other than a religious doctrine of salvation, with the sole difference that this time a meaning for life was derived not from a speculative belief in redemption but rather from a speculative interpretation of history. But a person who is honest with themselves has no more of a right to use historical ideology to avoid recognizing the world's absurdity than they do to use suicide or religious faith to do so. None of these three methods of evading absurdity are permissible because absurdity is a fundamental life-condition:

> It is a matter of living in that state of the absurd.[32]

We are now approaching the core of Camus' philosophy. What he calls on us to do, in fact, is to develop a new attitude toward life such as will enable us to exist in what he calls the "climate of absurdity".

Honesty with Oneself in the Face of Absurdity

One must, then, hold to the atmosphere of absurdity and even cultivate it. And once the climate of absurdity has gained its full density we find ourselves before the all-decisive question:

> Is one going to die, escape by the leap, rebuild a mansion of ideas and forms to one's own scale? Or is one, on the contrary, going to take up the heartrending and marvellous wager of the absurd? Let's make a final effort in this regard and draw all our conclusions. The body, affection, creation, action, human nobility will then resume their places in this mad world.[33]

If Man, then, does indeed take up this "wager of the absurd" and bets everything on pushing on even in the face of meaninglessness, he restores thereby, in the end, its dignity to a life that appeared to have been rendered valueless. Man can even become happy as he does so:

> From the moment absurdity is recognized, it becomes a passion, the most harrowing of all.[34]

The human being, then, who has been enlightened as to absurdity is in no way a frustrated individual who sits in a corner, apathetic and resigned to his fate; rather, he lives life as a passionate struggle and does not let himself be discouraged by the strains and stresses of life. To accept the challenge means, for Camus, to struggle resolutely against the randomness and chaos of the world:

> The absurd has meaning only in so far as it is not agreed to.[35]

This statement reveals the very crux of Camus' philosophy. The meaninglessness and chaos of the world are indeed a fact, as is our desire for clarity, order and predictability. But we would be wrong to take this factual contradiction as grounds for despair. On the contrary, it is with the recognition of these facts that there should begin what Camus calls our daily "revolt". In defiance of this meaninglessness we must get up every morning, perform our daily work, and apply all our strength to the task of continuing to live. Camus himself, for example, had two children, was a loving father, and also politically very active. But what, then, is it that distinguishes the man whom Camus calls "the absurd man", the man who has internalized the meaninglessness of existence, from the so-called "normal man"? Firstly, it is the fact that someone who has undergone the profound experience of absurdity is thenceforth unable to forget it:

A man who has become conscious of the absurd is forever bound to it.[36]

Secondly, the "absurd man" lives more freely, because he is no longer a slave to the future. He remains subject, indeed, to the same constraints as other people, but now he knows of these constraints. He recognizes the absurdity of his own actions but does not allow himself to be discouraged by this. On the contrary, he draws his strength and greatness from just this recognition:

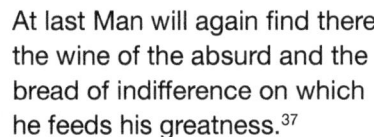

At last Man will again find there the wine of the absurd and the bread of indifference on which he feeds his greatness.[37]

What, concretely, does Camus want to convey with this poetic metaphor "the bread of indifference"? How exactly are we to envisage the "absurd man"'s attitude to life? It is the life of a figure belonging to Greek mythology, Sisyphus, that Camus uses in order to make concrete and clear to us the core of his philosophy.

The Myth of Sisyphus

The picture of Sisyphus given us by the poet Homer is a colourful and somewhat dubious one. He tells us that he was a character so zestful, headstrong and crafty that he showed no respect even to the gods. Thus, on one occasion he happened to witness Zeus's abduction of the beautiful daughter of the river-god Asopus; when Asopus began, after a while, to search for his missing daughter, Sisyphus dared to reveal to him the place where Zeus, the all-powerful father of all the Olympians, had hidden her; having recovered his daughter, the river-god rewarded Sisyphus by causing a spring to flow on the acropolis of Corinth, the city over which Sisyphus ruled as king.

Zeus, angry at Sisyphus's betrayal, then sent Thanatos, the personification of Death, to seize him. But the cunning King Sisyphus succeeded in making Death so drunk with wine that he was able to tie him up and prevent him from performing his office of fetching those destined to die. Only when Ares, the god of war, noticed with amazement that nobody was any longer dying on the battlefield, was the game finally up for Sisyphus. The war-god now went looking for Death, freed him, and dragged Sisyphus down into the Underworld, where he was harshly punished by the gods.

They set him to pushing, through all eternity, a heavy rock up to the summit of a steep-sloped mountain and ensured that this rock would always, just before Sisyphus had pushed it to the top, escape his grip and roll back down to the bottom once again. The gods, in other words, set for the headstrong, cunning and proud King Sisyphus a task that he could never complete and whose meaninglessness was to torment him forever more. It is precisely this absurd situation – that Sisyphus is condemned to pursue a goal that he knows he can never achieve – that makes him, for Camus, the darkly luminous role model for all those who have become aware of the essential absurdity of life:

> Sisyphus is the absurd hero. He is, as much through his passions as through his torture.[38]

Thus Camus compares the punishment of Sisyphus with the situation of the modern factory worker. Just as Sisyphus must, every day, roll his rock up the mountain, the worker on the production line must, every day over and over again, perform the same motions without recognizing any real purpose therein or any end in sight:

> The workman of today works every day in his life at the same tasks and this fate is no less absurd (than Sisyphus's). But it is tragic only at the rare moments when it becomes conscious.[39]

Sisyphus has, as compared to the modern workman, the additional problem that he is conscious at every second of the utter pointlessness of his action. And yet he does not give up. He neither despairs of his task nor begs the gods for mercy. No, he does not repent. On the contrary, he stands by his life and all that he did in it. It never, indeed, even occurs to him to give up. Although he well knows how vain all his effort will be, he continues, as if to spite and scorn the gods, to push with stoic indifference his rock up the slope of the mountain. For, as Camus writes:

> There is no fate that cannot be surmounted by scorn [...]. All Sisyphus's silent joy is contained therein. His fate belongs to him. His rock is his thing.[40]

Sisyphus, then, makes the dire situation that he has landed up in into his own situation, his own "thing". By resolutely deciding to persevere in this permanent rolling of a rock up a mountainside he preserves his dignity and his pride. Sisyphus is thereby, for Camus, the original and archetypal image of "Man in revolt": the human being who even in the face of the absurdity of existence does not give up but defiantly continues with his life. This is why the often-quoted final sentence of Camus' essay on *The Myth of Sisyphus* runs:

> One must imagine Sisyphus happy.[41]

Rebellion as an Attitude to Life

Camus summons us, then, to a permanent revolt or rebellion (in his second great philosophical statement, *The Rebel*, it is the term "rebellion" that we find used where *The Myth of Sisyphus* had mostly used "revolt") against that offensive strain upon our sensibility that is the meaninglessness of human existence:

> Metaphysical rebellion is the movement by which Man protests against his condition and against the whole of creation.[42]

Concretely, this means simply to get up every morning and go to work even if one cannot see any reason to do so (aside from the material remuneration one gets for it). But this word "rebellion" does in fact also have a political and moral significance in Camus' work that goes beyond the mere stoic persistence in a meaningless life. Thus it is important, for example, to resist clear injustice and to set limits:

> What is a rebel? A man who says 'no'. [...] What does he mean by saying 'no'? He means, for example, that 'this has been going on too long', 'up to this point, yes; beyond it, no', 'you are going too far' or, again, 'there is a limit beyond which you shall not go'.[43]

The mere fact that we cannot recognize any meaning inhering in the world as its ordering and guiding principle does not mean that we must stay passive and apolitical. Camus makes it unmistakably clear in his book *The Rebel* that one must never simply accept what is wrong and unjust:

> Unless we choose to ignore reality, we must find our values in it.[44]

Camus' Central Idea

This further step in Camus' thinking is at first hard to comprehend. How can it be that Camus is now suddenly concerned with justice and moral values? If the world is absurd, unpredictable and dependent on mere chance alone, then surely it must be a matter of indifference whether what happens in it is just or unjust. But Camus does not subscribe to such a line of reasoning. He argues rather that a person most definitely can, while recognizing that life is absurd, still engage in a search for moral values. The world is indeed chaotic and contradictory; but this does not prevent anyone from trying to create just conditions within his immediate human environment. Because everyone – so argues Camus – has within himself a reliable sense of what is just and what is unjust:

He opposes the principle of justice which he finds in himself to the principle of injustice which he sees being applied in the world.[45]

Wherever the experience of the "absurd man" encounters suffering, rebellion becomes a duty. He must be careful, however, not to lapse into ideological tyranny and impose, by violence, his own ideas about justice and injustice on other people.

It is at this point that Camus draws a key distinction between "rebellion" and "revolution". "Revolution", as the communists so influential in his day conceived of it, Camus condemned as contemptuous of humanity. He was, for example, a harsh critic of what "revolution" had quickly led to in the Soviet Union. The party leader Stalin, he pointed out, was using the notion of a "goal of human history" – imagined to be a kind of paradise lying somewhere in the future – to terrorise, murder or throw into work-camps thousands of human beings who really existed in the here and now.

It is the distinguishing mark of Camus' "rebel", however, that he respects, in his "rebellion", *actually and presently* lived human life and concerns himself with the needs and sorrows of human beings in just that "here and now" that the "revolutionary" tends to ride roughshod over in the name of the glorious future. "Rebellion" then, as Camus understands it, is something that limits itself to the sphere of direct personal experience:

Camus' Central Idea

> This is why (rebellion) relies primarily on the most concrete realities – on a person's occupation; on the village, where the living heart of things and of men is to be found.[46]

Sartre criticized Camus' idea of "rebellion" as a form of resistance rooted in the personal and concrete as a naïve, "un-political" conception. It was of the very essence of politics, Sartre argued, to organize on a larger scale and to attempt to achieve something globally by a broad collective effort that set long-term goals. Camus himself, indeed, had joined, as a young man of twenty-one, the Communist Party of Algeria but left it again five years later in 1937 after fundamental disagreements with its policies. From that time on he remained a declared opponent of the politics of violent overthrow. His break with Sartre, who remained on into the post-war years a defender of Soviet Communism, was played out in the columns of Sartre's magazine *Les Temps Modernes*. The former friends never spoke again. But Camus held to his view that, given the absurdity of the world, it is dangerously arrogant to try to define utopian political goals for a distant future. Modern man, he said, must know his limits:

> And so the real drama of revolutionary thought is announced. In order to exist, Man must rebel, but rebellion must respect the limit it discovers in itself [...].[47]

Of What Use is Camus' Discovery for Us Today?

Living With Absurdity – Freeing Oneself from Bourgeois Rules of Conduct

Camus surely discovered, with his "climate of absurdity", a phenomenon which all of us have at one time or another encountered. There is probably no one who has not at some point in his or her life, for a shorter or longer period, undergone this experience of the absurd. The death of a relative or friend, or the ending of a long-standing love-relationship, can cause one's whole familiar world to collapse like a house of cards. One falls into a deep hole and is forced to recognize that the feeling of enduring safety and protectedness that one had enjoyed had only been an illusion. The familiar world suddenly becomes cold and threatening. A chasm opens up between our wish for integration and our actual helpless exposure to the chaos of the world.

Camus' philosophy offers at least the small comfort of portraying this gulf between our wishes and reality not as some personal failing or culpability on our own part but as a consequence of the existential situation of Man in the world. Man has a natural disposition to seek meaning and a sense of protectedness but must, at regular intervals, discover that neither is to be found in the world. Camus brings home to us the fact that this contradiction inheres in the very essence of Man. Since Man wishes to understand his world, he is obliged – unlike, say, a plant – to constantly interpret it:

If I were a tree among trees, a cat among animals, this life would have a meaning, or rather this problem would not arise, for I should belong to this world.[48]

Unlike the tree, Man needs to find his place in the world. Together with others, he begins, right from the day he is born, to understand the world and to take up a position within it. Thus, already as a small child he develops wishes, begins to form plans, and to dream of a future for himself. Once he has grown up, he is able to start fully structuring the course of his days and weeks, his holidays, his wedding etc. and to make the attempt to bring his life completely under his control. Relationships, marriage, children, job, and living situation play a great role here because they bring solidity to a human life. But this innate striving for order – and this is Camus' key idea – necessarily sooner or later encounters its limit. However well and reasonably one may plan out one's life, there will always be unexpected turns of events, catastrophes, windfalls, separations and new encounters which will cause all one's careful plans to go awry. What is more, the fact that we all have to die in the end puts all our projects, however good, radically into question. Our mind strives for order, constancy, and a firm future; but the world is chaotic, uncertain, and overshadowed by mortality:

That evidence is the absurd. It is that divorce between the mind that desires and the world that disappoints.[49]

Camus recommends that we do not attempt to block out the absurd but rather allow ourselves to experience it and even consciously hold to it:

> If, therefore, I want to preserve it, I can, through a constant awareness, ever revived, ever alert. This is what, for the moment, I must remember. At this moment, the absurd, so obvious and yet so hard to win, returns to a man's life and finds its home there.[50]

The absurd, then, ought to "find a home" in our lives. This means nothing other than that we should live in a constant and thorough awareness of the absurd. Sisyphus too rolls his rock up the mountain again and again, even though he knows that it will always roll back down. He could give up and resign himself, but he continues with his senseless labour in order to show the gods that their punishment cannot debase him. This is the true meaning of the "rebellion" to which Camus repeatedly exhorts us. Man must withstand absurdity, rebel against it, and continue, proud and upright, with his life. When the alarm clock rings in the morning, the "absurd man" should get up like everybody else, go to work, earn his living, buy the goods he needs, eat, drink etc. The only difference between his life and that of the "normal" man is that the "absurd man" is conscious at every moment of the contradictory nature of his existence. The "absurd man" is also aware of how limited the time he has to live actually is. This insight, however, leads to a profound sense of freedom:

> [...] Completely turned toward death (taken here as the most obvious absurdity), the absurd man feels released from everything outside that passionate attention crystallizing in him. He enjoys a freedom with regard to common rules.[51]

That human being who accepts absurdity and lives with it will comply, as regards the rules and laws of the society he lives in, only with those which he himself judges to be right. In this way Camus sharpens our perception of what is truly essential and encourages us to follow our own path(s). The man who simply complies with what he has been told, taught and commanded to do ever since his childhood is unfree: a slave to an account of the world that has been handed down to him. But the man who accepts the need to recognize the absurdity of the world and to live with this absurdity will stand by nothing except that which he himself, at any given time, considers to be right, and is able to measure the whole world by this standard.

Absurd Lifestyles: Actors and Seducers

But what does this mean concretely? How exactly must one envisage a life that is led in full awareness of the fact that existence is constantly changing and irredeemably finite? Camus provides us with some easily-grasped examples of "the absurd lifestyle".

An actor, for example, has no choice but to adopt an absurd attitude to life if he wishes to do his job in a truly professional manner. This is so inasmuch as he must fully identify, over and over again, with his roles. That is to say, he must, through a creative act, make the characters he plays come alive. He tries to feel, think and behave as these characters would and, in the end, transforms himself into them completely. And when the performance is over he must, as it were, let his character "die" in order that he can slip into some new persona. Camus interprets this as follows:

> It requires but a little imagination to feel what an actor's fate means. It is in time that he makes up and enumerates his characters. It is in time likewise that he learns to dominate them. The greater number of different lives he has lived the more aloof he can be from them.[52]

Just as Sisyphus tirelessly rolls his rock up the mountain, knowing that he does so in vain, the actor breathes, with all his passion, life into characters whom he knows will soon die or be forgotten, even despite the brief vitality that he infuses into them:

> By thus sweeping over centuries and minds, by miming Man as he can be and as he is, the actor has much in common with that other absurd individual, the traveller. Like him, he drains something and is constantly on the move.[53]

Another example that Camus gives us of the "absurd lifestyle" is the fate of the legendary seducer Don Juan. He conquers the heart of woman after woman and indeed falls in love himself with each one. But he cannot stay with any of them. He never marries or settles down but loves and lives only for the moment of seduction. Since such behaviour does not accord with the moral rules applying in his era, he is pursued and persecuted by the authorities and by the church but even this does not prevent him making further conquests. And yet, Camus suggests, such a lifestyle really isn't anything so special, since in the end:

> He is an ordinary seducer. Except for the difference that he is conscious and that is why he is absurd.[54]

Don Juan lives absurdly for two reasons. Firstly, he trusts solely to his own sense of reality in the here and now and professes an idea of fulfilled love that is personal to him. The rules of the world around him seem to him to be without meaning for his own self and his inner nature. Secondly, he is aware already at the start of every one of his passionate love-relationships that he will never achieve fulfilment in the form of an absolute and eternal love. It would be a mistake, Camus argues, to believe that Don Juan was only a dreamer searching for some "total love"; someone who had sought this on and on, restlessly and desperately, but never found what he was looking for. Rather, Don Juan was fully aware that every love is a fleeting, perishable thing. Thus Camus tells us of how, when a woman who hoped she had won him for herself alone exclaimed with delight: "At last I have given you love!", Don Juan replied, laughing: "At last? No. But once more!" Don Juan's "love" is a love of the intensity of the moment; he must seek this moment again and again, just as Sisyphus pushes his rock again and again up the mountain. But this does not make Don Juan's love a bad or immoral one. Because, as Camus says:

> Why should it be essential to love rarely in order to love much? [55]

Don Juan loves and desires each time with all his heart. It is this that makes him so irresistible for women. Since what is holy for him is love, he must experience it again and again in its whole intensity, in order then to lose it again. This, says Camus, is what makes Don Juan's love something special:

Of What Use is Camus' Discovery for Us Today?

> There is no noble love but that which recognizes itself to be both short-lived and exceptional. All those deaths and all those rebirths gathered together as in a sheaf make up for Don Juan the flowering of his life.[56]

Both Don Juan and the actor are absurd heroes because they surrender themselves unconditionally, over and over, to their passion. When they seduce a woman or bring, in an authentic way, a character onto the stage, they feel alive. But they know at the same time that they will not be able to preserve this sense of vitality. It repeatedly slips away from them and they must begin again from the start. But just this is a symbol for a life lived intensely in full awareness of absurdity.

Finding the "Golden Mean"

But how are we to find our way to such an intensely lived life if we are neither actors nor great seducers?

If one considers the "absurd lifestyles" specifically pointed to by Camus along with his exhortation to live a life of "permanent rebellion", the conclusion to be drawn is that his philosophy urges on us an attitude to life that is resolutely focussed upon the moment or the present. One must stand by one's own passion. This passion can also take the form of a political commitment. What can be done here must be done; but ideological thoughts of a future total salvation of mankind must be rejected. This is why Camus places right at the start of his principal work of philosophy a quotation from the Greek poet Pindar that points out the direction his thoughts will follow:

O my soul, do not aspire to immortal life, but exhaust the limits of the possible.[57]

The individual human being has to prove himself, day by day, in the face of the absurd. It is Camus' view that he can best do this by finding a middle path between total debauchery and a stoic self-abandonment to the fact of death. This fact that we all have to die one day must not tip us into a panic over the possibility that today could be our last day and prompt us to ruthlessly and egotistically taste of all the world has to offer. But it likewise makes no sense to orient one's life-project toward some vision of the future which may never become a reality and whose actual benenfits cannot even be accurately assessed. Even when one lives with passion, the "golden mean" must be found and respected:

In order to exist, Man must rebel, but rebellion must respect the limit it discovers in itself [...]. 58

The motto, therefore, of the "absurd man" is neither "Seize the day!" nor "Always think ahead!" Both contradict, in Camus' view, the good Mediterranean attitude toward life which consists in respecting the "golden mean". Take, for example, the issue of making provision for one's old age. Of course it makes sense to take steps to ensure one will still live well then; but it makes no sense at all to live one's whole life thinking only of one's retirement and acting always with a view to these last years. To "live with absurdity" means, for Camus, to learn to use the lack of transparency of our absurd existence as an opportunity to make, within the limits of our immediate human environment, the changes that seem to us just and good to make. Permanent rebellion must be part of our life. Constant revolt against injustice belongs as much to the "absurd lifestyle" as does the intense surrender of oneself to the pleasure of the moment.

Composure in the Face of Life's Unpredictability

If it is indeed the case, as Camus insists, that the world is ruled by chance and our lives marked by a chain of unforeseeable circumstances and eventualities, and if no higher meaning is to be identified by which these eventualities can be ordered as more or less important, then all experiences are of equal value. And Camus does in fact defend the view that all life-experiences are of equal value, so that it is not the quality of individual experiences but only their quantity that matters. Thus, a long life is to be preferred to a short one:

> For, on the one hand, the absurd teaches that all experiences are unimportant and, on the other, it urges toward the greatest quantity of experiences.[59]

For this reason, not even a very full life, if it proves to be short, can ever make up for the loss of that enormous treasure of experience that would have been comprised in a longer one:

> Thus it is that no depth, no emotion, no passion, and no sacrifice could render equal in the eyes of the absurd man (even if he wished it so) a conscious life of forty years and a lucidity spread over sixty years.[60]

A long life is thus in every case a boon, and a short one always an enormous loss. Camus writes:

> To the actor as to the absurd man, a premature death is irreparable. Nothing can make up for the sum of faces and centuries he would otherwise have traversed.[61]

Of What Use is Camus' Discovery for Us Today?

It seems all the more tragic, then, that Camus, who stressed in this way, in many passages of his work, the importance of a long life, died suddenly and prematurely, at the age of 46, in a car crash.

His death remains a mysterious one, not because its circumstances were in any way unclear – on the contrary, all the details are known very precisely – but because a series of absurd coincidences played decisive roles in it.

Camus spent Christmas that year with his family in his country house in Provence. Since his two children were to return to school right after the holidays, his plan was to travel with them and his wife back to Paris on the 2nd of January 1960. He had already bought four train tickets when the family of his friend Michel Gallimard (nephew of his publisher) made a surprise visit. Gallimard proposed to Camus that he let his wife and children go on ahead and drive back with him two days later. Camus hesitated but agreed.

Two days later he was sitting in the front passenger seat next to Gallimard, who was driving, when the car veered off the road and smashed head-on into a plane tree. Camus and Gallimard were killed. Gallimard's own wife and daughter, seated in the back, were thrown clear, miraculously surviving unscathed.

Camus' own unused railway ticket was found in his pocket. Already years before Camus had written:

> Man does not choose. The absurd and the extra life it involves *therefore do not depend on Man's will*, but on its contrary, which is death. Weighing words carefully, it is altogether a question of luck.[62]

Of what use to us today, then, are Camus' ideas about "the absurd"? The question is hard to answer. He recommends a long life, but also writes that we do not ourselves have any influence over this. As a way of facing the unpredictability and absurdity of life he urges upon us composure and a conduct that respects the "golden mean". But on the other hand he refers us to the intensity and passion of the absurd hero Don Juan and exhorts us to permanent rebellion. Camus' philosophy of the absurd remains, still today, a philosophy of diverse and shifting implications. What can we take from it that is of use in our modern life? In what respects can we say that Camus was and is right?

Let us hold to this key image of Sisyphus. Camus certainly recognized and brought to light an uncomfortable truth here: modern Man really is in many respects confronted with a situation much like Sisyphus's. He must do his duty every day over and over, mastering the demands of everyday existence, without ever really understanding what sense there may be to such a life. Most people today no longer believe in God, nor do they believe in "the sacred fatherland" or other such ideological political visions. Modern society therefore lacks things to hold onto and is constantly facing a structural crisis of meaning. We also see economic, financial and environmental catastrophes which are increasingly shaking people's confidence that even their material security can be preserved.

All this being the case, Camus' diagnosis of an "absurd existence" certainly remains relevant today. But the most valuable thing he hands down to us is his discovery of the opportunities that are opened up by such an existence. Thus, the end of church and politics as sources of sense and meaning can also be looked upon as a liberation. The collapse of the religious and political tutelage once exerted by Christianity, nationalism and communism has enabled millions of people for the first time to comprehend and transform their worlds on the basis of their own impulses and aspirations. We should seize this opportunity. Because – and this is Camus's true legacy to us – every human being can, through a "rebellion" persisted in day after day, join in the work of building a more just world. Even if the universe, in Camus' view, remains an uncomprehended mystery and we can see no end to our ever-repeated efforts, the task that we are engaged in is nonetheless a rewarding one:

One must imagine Sisyphus happy.[63]

Bibliographical References:

1. Albert Camus, The Myth of Sisyphus (translated by Justin O'Brien) Penguin Modern Classics, 2000, p. 10.
2. Ibid. p. 31
3. Albert Camus, Notebooks 1935 – 42, (translated by Philip Thody), Knopf Books, 1963, pps. 137 - 138
4. Albert Camus, The Myth of Sisyphus, p. 17
5. Ibid. p. 40
6. Ibid. pps. 11 - 12
7. Ibid. p. 13
8. Ibid. p. 12 - 13
9. Ibid. p. 10
10. Ibid. p. 13
11. Ibid. p. 13
12. Ibid. p. 11
13. Ibid. p. 7
14. Ibid. p. 15
15. Ibid. p. 37
16. Ibid. p. 17
17. Ibid. p. 12
18. Ibid. p. 17
19. Ibid. p. 5
20. Ibid. p. 7
21. Ibid. p. 41
22. Ibid. p. 40
23. Ibid.
24. Ibid.
25. Ibid. p. 41
26. Ibid. pps. 30-31
27. Ibid. p. 38
28. Ibid. p. 42
29. Ibid.
30. Ibid. p. 8
31. Albert Camus, The Rebel, An Essay on Man in Revolt, Vintage International Edition, 1991, p. 298

32 Albert Camus, The Myth of Sisyphus (translated by Justin O'Brien) Penguin Modern Classics, 2000, p. 31
33 Ibid. p. 39
34 Ibid. p. 18
35 Ibid. p. 25
36 Ibid.
37 Ibid. p. 39
38 Ibid. p. 87
39 Ibid.
40 Ibid. p. 88
41 Ibid. p. 89
42 Albert Camus, The Rebel, An Essay on Man in Revolt, Vintage International Edition, 1991, p. 23
43 Ibid. p. 13
44 Ibid. p. 21
45 Ibid. p. 24
46 Ibid. p. 298
47 Ibid. p. 22
48 Albert Camus, The Myth of Sisyphus (translated by Justin O'Brien) Penguin Modern Classics, 2000, p. 39
49 Ibid. p. 37
50 Ibid. p. 39
51 Ibid. p. 44
52 Ibid. p. 61
53 Ibid. p. 58
54 Ibid. p. 53
55 Ibid. p. 51
56 Ibid. p. 54
57 Ibid. p. vii
58 Albert Camus, The Rebel, An Essay on Man in Revolt, Vintage International Edition, 1991, p. 22
59 Albert Camus, The Myth of Sisyphus (translated by Justin O'Brien) Penguin Modern Classics, 2000, p. 46
60 Ibid. p. 47
61 Ibid. p. 61
62 Ibid. p. 47
63 Ibid. p. 89

Already published in the same series:

Walther Ziegler
Camus in 60 Minutes
ISBN 9783741227738

Walther Ziegler
Freud in 60 Minutes
ISBN 9783741227707

Walther Ziegler
Hegel in 60 Minutes
ISBN 9783741227677

Walther Ziegler
Heidegger in 60 Minutes
ISBN 9783741227752

Walther Ziegler
Kant in 60 Minutes
ISBN 9783741226373

Walther Ziegler
Marx in 60 Minutes
ISBN 9783741227691

Walther Ziegler
Platon in 60 Minutes
ISBN 9783741227615

Walther Ziegler
Rousseau in 60 Minutes
ISBN 9783741227622

Walther Ziegler
Sartre in 60 Minutes
ISBN 9783741227653

Walther Ziegler
Smith in 60 Minutes
ISBN 9783741227721

Coming soon in the same series:

Walther Ziegler
Adorno in 60 Minutes

Walther Ziegler
Arendt in 60 Minutes

Walther Ziegler
Bacon in 60 Minutes

Walther Ziegler
Descartes in 60 Minutes

Walther Ziegler
Foucault in 60 Minutes

Walther Ziegler
Habermas in 60 Minutes

Walther Ziegler
Hobbes in 60 Minutes

Walther Ziegler
Nietzsche in 60 Minutes

Walther Ziegler
Popper in 60 Minutes

Walther Ziegler
Rawls in 60 Minutes

Walther Ziegler
Schopenhauer in 60 Minutes

Walther Ziegler
Wittgenstein in 60 Minutes

The author:

Dr Walther Ziegler is academically trained in the fields of philosophy, history and political science. As a foreign correspondent, reporter and newsroom coordinator for the German TV station ProSieben he has produced films on every continent. His news reports have won several prizes and awards. He has also authored numerous books in the field of philosophy. His many years of experience as a journalist mean that he is able to present the complex ideas of the great philosophers in a way that is both engaging and very clear. Since 2007 he has also been active as a teacher and trainer of young TV journalists in Munich, holding the post of Academic Director at the Media Academy, an institute of higher education that offers film and TV courses at its base directly on the site of the major European film production company Bavaria Film.